Zoo Animals

Children's Nature Library

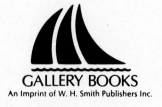

GALLERY BOOKS
An Imprint of W. H. Smith Publishers Inc.

Louis Weber, C.E.O.
Publications International, Ltd.
7373 North Cicero Avenue
Lincolnwood, Illinois 60646

Permission is never granted for commercial
purposes.

Printed in U.S.A.

8 7 6 5 4 3 2 1

ISBN 0-8317-6472-4

This edition published in 1991 by Gallery Books,
an imprint of W.H. Smith Publishers, Inc., 112
Madison Avenue, New York, New York 10016.

Gallery Books are available for bulk purchase for
sales and promotions and premium use. For
details write or telephone the Manager of Special
Sales, W.H. Smith Publishers, Inc., 112 Madison
Avenue, New York, New York 10016;
(212) 532-6600.

Written by Eileen Spinelli

Credits:
Animals/Animals: Doug Allan: 36; Fran Allan: 20,
28; Henry Ausloos: 10, 32; M. Austerman: 16, 22,
32, 34, 35, 54; Anthony Bannister: 8, 10; G.I.
Bernard: 9; Hans & Judy Beste: 30; Mike
Birkhead: 58; John Chellman: 16, 17, 33; Ken
Cole: 30, 31, 61; Margot Conte: 24, 36, 46; Pat
Crowe: 19; E.R. Degginger: 20, 23, 51; Michael
Dick: 6, 34, 48; Harry Engels: 40; Michael
Fogden: 57; David C. Fritts: 29, 46; Adrienne T.
Gibson: 14, 50; Mickey Gibson: 13, 22, 44, 50;
Arthur Gloor: 54, 55; Johnny Johnson: 47; Kevin
Johnson: 56; Susan Jones: 22, 38; Breck P. Kent:
49; Richard Kolar: 5, 11, 42; G.L. Kooyman: 36,
37; Zig Leszczynski: 8, 18, 25, 26, 27, 34, 39, 45,
56, 60; Bates Littlehales: 15; Robert A. Lubeck:
52; Willard Luce: 58; Joe McDonald: 6, 7; Stefan
Meyers: 10; Terry G. Murphy: 28; Patti Murray: 14,
38; Charles Palek: 52, 53; Ralph A. Reinhold: 18,
48, 62; L.L.T. Rhodes: 16, 43, 44; J.H. Robinson:
40; Alen Rokah: 59; Leonard Lee Rue, III: 54, 60,
62; Anup & Manoj Shah: 24, 28; Souricat: 41;
Stouffer Ent., Inc.: 46; Alfred B. Thomas: 20; Jim
Tuten: 3, 42. **Earth Scenes:** Margot Conte: 4; J.C.
Stevenson: 4. **Gerry Ellis Wildlife:** 12.
International Stock: Jim Cambon: 62; N.
Ledbetter: 63; Ronn Muratea: 20, 21, Back Cover;
Will Regan: 32; Spencer: 62. **National
Geographic:** Front Cover, 1.

Table of Contents

Introduction 4
Elephant 8
Hippopotamus 10
Crocodile 12
Giraffe 14
Gorilla 16
Rhinoceros 18
Zebra 20
Camel 22
Lion 24
Tiger 26
Cheetah 28
Kangaroo 30
Chimpanzee 32
Monkey 34
Penguin 36
Llama 38
Moose 40
Flamingo 42
Dolphin 44
Polar Bear 46
Giant Panda 48
Koala 50
Black Bear 52
Ostrich 54
Snake 56
Peacock 58
Walrus 60
Seal 62

Introduction

The first zoo was built about 3,000 years ago in Egypt. Since that time, people in many other countries have also kept zoos. Five hundred years ago, there was a zoo in Mexico that had special bronze cages for animals and basins for fish. There were also hundreds of zookeepers and special nurses to care for sick animals. The first zoo in the United States was built in Philadelphia in 1854.

All zoos used to keep animals in cages. Some still do. But many zoos give animals a home that looks like their natural environment. This kind of zoo is called a habitat zoo. In these zoos, you find jungles, rain forests, grasslands, and even polar islands. Animals that live together in the wild are often kept together in a habitat zoo. Scientists believe that animals are happier and healthier in habitat zoos.

Introduction

In the wild, animals must hunt for food. But zoos provide special diets for the animals. Some zoos serve fresh foods—hay, grain, fruit, vegetables, chicken, meat, and fish. Others use dry foods much like those you feed your cat or dog. Unless the zoo permits you to feed the animals, you should never offer a zoo animal any kind of food.

Zoos care about the health and happiness of animals everywhere. Some zoos take in injured wild animals. Some zoos protect endangered animals, and all zoos encourage us to support efforts to help animals live happily in their natural homes.

When you visit the zoo, remember that it is the animals' home. Don't tease the animals. Put your gum wrapper and other litter in a waste can. And take time to learn about the animals you see.

Elephant

The elephant is the largest animal that lives on land. In just one day, an elephant can eat 500 pounds of hay. It can also drink 60 gallons of water. The elephant has an amazing nose called a trunk. Can you pick up food with your nose? Can you give yourself a shower with your nose? Can you make your nose sound like a very loud trumpet? An elephant can.

Gorilla

Gorillas may look fierce, but they are very gentle. A young gorilla has black fur. As it gets older, its fur turns gray. Gorillas eat fruit and leaves. They do not like baths. Mother gorilla builds her nest in the trees. She and her baby sleep in the nest. Father gorilla makes a soft bed on the ground. He guards the nest.

Rhinoceros

The rhinoceros has an unusual horn on its snout. It is really not a horn at all but tightly matted hair. Sometimes a rhino's horn is torn off in a fight. No problem. It will grow back. The rhinoceros loves to swim and take mud baths. It likes to eat at night and in the early morning. After a meal, the rhinoceros will find a nice cool spot and sleep for the rest of the day.

Zebra

A zebra's stripes make it look like a horse wearing a tiger costume. Zebras are excellent runners. A herd of hundreds of zebras can run close together and never trip over each other. The zebra loves to scratch. It scratches against large rocks, against trees, and even against another zebra. If the itch is very hard to reach, the zebra rolls in the dust.

Camel

In desert countries, camels carry heavy burdens for people. They can go for days without food and water. Camels can walk across sand without sinking into it. Their thick, curly eyelashes protect their eyes from blowing sand. Some camels have one hump. Other camels have two humps. Camels are not friendly. They often fight with each other. Don't dare annoy a camel—it will spit at you.

Lion

The lion is clever, powerful, and quick. Male lions have thick manes. They like to spend time alone. Female lions do most of the hunting. They are also good mothers. They are patient and loving to their cubs. Lions take catnaps throughout the day. If you want to hear a lion roar, you'll have to wait until it is dark. Most lions that live in zoos are friendly and playful—if you know how to handle them.

Tiger

Tigers are the largest and strongest cats. They live in mountains, swamps, and forests. Their stripes blend in with the shadows, so it's hard to see them. A tiger doesn't like hot weather. On a hot day, it may stay in a cool cave or hide in the thick grass. Tigers love the water and go swimming whenever they can. Like lions, tigers hunt at night.

Cheetah

The cheetah runs faster than any other animal. Its top speed is about 60 miles per hour. But there's a problem: The cheetah can't run this fast for very long. It gets tired quickly. The cheetah is not good at climbing trees, and it doesn't fight very well. When a cheetah is angry, it shows its teeth and snarls. When it is contented, it purrs just like your cat at home.

Kangaroo

The kangaroo carries her baby around with her in a pouch. Animals that have special pouches for their young are called marsupial (mahr-SOO-pee-uhl). Kangaroos eat plants and drink very little water. They like to bathe in rivers. Fortunately, kangaroos don't wear clothes because they continue to grow larger during their entire lives. There are more then 50 different kinds of kangaroos. You are most likely to see a gray kangaroo at the zoo.

Chimpanzee

The chimpanzee is one of the smartest animals. It can use tools. Chimpanzees use rocks to crack nuts. They use sticks to get honey from beehives, and they use long blades of grass to fish for termites. In the wild, chimpanzees travel in groups. At night, the whole family snuggles in the treetops. In the zoo, chimpanzees are friendly, curious, and playful.

Monkey

African black and white monkeys

Monkeys look like animal acrobats when they swing on the bars and leap from place to place. Some monkeys swing by their tails as well as their paws. In the wild, monkeys live together in large families. Some monkeys make their homes in the trees; others prefer to live on the ground. Monkeys usually eat fruit and plants, but sometimes they eat insects, birds, and eggs.

Diana monkeys

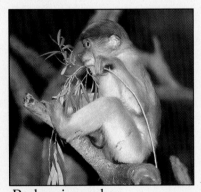

Proboscis monkey

White cheeked gibbon ▶

Penguin

Peruvian penguin

Emperor penguin

Penguins live in the southern half of the world. They are very good at swimming and diving, but they can't fly. A penguin's wings are like flippers. On land, penguins waddle on their short legs. Sometimes they slide across the ice on their bellies. Their favorite food is fish. The largest penguin is four feet tall; it is the emperor penguin. The king penguin is the second largest penguin.

Emperor penguin

King penguins ▶

Llama

The llama looks a lot like a big, tall sheep. Its light-brown fur can be made into yarn. Llamas are used as pack animals, but they move slowly and can carry no more than 100 pounds. Llamas are also stubborn. They will lie down on the trail and refuse to get up. But they can walk easily along high, narrow mountain ledges. When a llama is angry, it spits.

Moose

The moose is the largest kind of deer. A moose's antlers are so big you could probably hang all your winter clothes on them. Moose live in the forest. They can walk through the woods without making a sound. But moose are not always quiet and peaceful. Males use their antlers to fight. Moose are good swimmers and love to eat water plants.

Flamingo

The flamingo is a tall, pink bird. It wades in shallow water. You can tell if a flamingo has been eating the right foods by the color of its feathers. If it is eating properly, its feathers will be pink. If it has a bad diet, its feathers will be dull white.

Flamingos build their nests with mud. The nest is shaped like a bowl so the eggs won't roll out.

Dolphin

Dolphins are small whales and breathe air. They have their own underwater language of sounds, clicks, and whistles. Dolphins eat fish, squid, and shrimp. At night, they sleep just below the surface of the water. Dolphins are playful. Sometimes they swim with people. In the zoo, dolphins can be trained to leap out of their tanks and do many kinds of tricks.

Polar Bear

The polar bear lives in the arctic where it is cold during most of the year. It has very long, thick fur that is snowy white. Polar bears love to swim and dive. They also like to slide on their bellies or backs down steep banks of snow. Even the grownups are playful. After a polar bear finishes eating, it cleans its paws just like a cat does.

Giant Panda

The giant panda comes to the zoo from China. It looks like a huge black-and-white teddy bear. But it may not be a bear at all. Some scientists think pandas are a kind of large raccoon. They eat only bamboo leaves and stems. Even though giant pandas are shy, they like to show off for people who visit them in the zoo. But some older pandas are cranky.

Koala

The koala looks like a cuddly baby bear. But it isn't a bear. It is a marsupial and carries its young in a pouch much like a kangaroo.
A koala has four hands and no feet, so it has a hard time getting around on the ground. But a koala moves easily through the trees. Koalas eat only one thing—the leaves of eucalyptus trees. They almost never need to drink water.

Black Bear

The black bear is especially good at climbing trees. It is so comfortable in the treetops that sometimes it takes a nap lying on a tree limb high above the ground. Black bears will eat animals, fish, pinecones, and berries. But their favorite food is honey. The black bear's thick hide protects it from beestings, so it can eat as much honey as it wants without worrying about the bees.

Ostrich

The ostrich is the biggest, tallest, and fastest bird in the world. It also lays the largest eggs. Ostriches are good swimmers, but they are much too heavy to fly.

Ostriches have stretchy throats. They swallow large plants and insects. They also swallow stones that help their digestion. Ostriches have swallowed pencils, locks, ropes, combs, and jewelry.

Snake

Bull snake

Snakes live on the ground, in trees, and in the water. They eat mice, frogs, rabbits, and other small animals. Some snakes also eat eggs and other snakes. You might think that snakes are slimy. But their skin is dry to the touch. You may also think that most snakes are poisonous. But there are only four kinds of poisonous snakes in the United States: Rattle snakes, copperheads, cottonmouth water moccasins, and coral snakes.

Red rat snake

Western ground snake

Coral snake ▶

Peacock

The peacock is one of the most beautiful birds in the zoo. Peacocks have bright blue or green feathers. When a peacock wants to show off for a peahen, it fans out its tail. Do you think that the spots on the peacock's tail look like eyes? Many people do. Peacocks roost in trees. They don't like crowds and prefer to be left alone by other birds and people.

Walrus

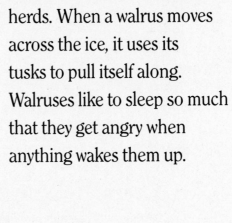

The walrus is awkward on land, but in the water it is a graceful swimmer. Walruses live in the arctic where it is very cold during most of the year. They stay together in herds. When a walrus moves across the ice, it uses its tusks to pull itself along. Walruses like to sleep so much that they get angry when anything wakes them up.

Seal

The seal is at home in the cold sea. A layer of fat known as blubber keeps the seal warm. It can even sleep under the water. But sometimes seals come onto shore to rest or sunbathe on the ice. They also have their babies on land. Instead of legs, seals have flippers to help them swim fast. They eat fish and shellfish.

Chimpanzee